THE BARKING THING

Suzanne Batty was born in Plymouth, 20 minutes after her twin sister, and upside down. Her family moved to suburban Manchester when she was two. She worked with young homeless people in London before studying English at Sussex University; she then worked variously as a gardener, a youth worker, a welfare rights advisor and suffered for several years as a civil servant. Although she has always written, Suzanne did not start writing poetry seriously until her 30s. She was one of the winners of the Poetry Business pamphlet competition in 1997 with *Shrink* (Smith/Doorstop, 1998), and received a writer's bursary from North West Arts in 1999. She is a founder member of urban poetry project The A6 Poets, and lives in Manchester, where she writes, teaches writing, performs her work, edits the poetry magazine *Rain Dog* and digs her allotment. She is also studying for an MA at Sheffield Hallam University..

SUZANNE BATTY

THE
BARKING
THING

To Barbara
hope you enjoy
The poems at your
leisure!
Suzanne Batty.

BLOODAXE BOOKS

Copyright © Suzanne Batty 2007

ISBN: 978 1 85224 772 0

First published 2007 by
Bloodaxe Books Ltd,
Highgreen,
Tarset,
Northumberland NE48 1RP.

www.bloodaxebooks.com
For further information about Bloodaxe titles
please visit our website or write to
the above address for a catalogue.

Bloodaxe Books Ltd acknowledges
the financial assistance of
Arts Council England, North East.

Cover design: Neil Astley & Pamela Robertson-Pearce.

Cover printing: J. Thomson Colour Printers Ltd, Glasgow.

Printed in Great Britain by
Bell & Bain Limited, Glasgow, Scotland.

This is for Joan.
And for my family,
not forgetting Storm.

ACKNOWLEDGEMENTS

Acknowledgements are due to the editors of the following publications, in which some of these poems first appeared: *Beyond Paradise* (Crocus Books, 1990), *Fat Chance, Iota, The Nerve: The 1998 Virago Book of Writing Women* (1998), *The North, Obsessed with Pipework, Other Poetry, Rain Dog, The Rialto, Road Works: Poems from the A6* (Panshine Press, 2004), *Smiths Knoll, Smoke* and *The Ugly Tree.*

Several of these poems appeared in a pamphlet, *Shrink* (Smith/Doorstop Books, 1998), winner of the Poetry Business pamphlet competition in 1997.

'Dog's gift' was originally commissioned by the Poems for the Waiting Room project by Rogan Wolf and David Hart, supported by Arts Council New Audiences funding in 2000.

'This horse' was written in response to *Golden Seas*, a painting by contemporary artist Linda Norris, and appeared in a catalogue of her work in 2001.

Thanks are due to North West Arts for a writer's bursary awarded in 1999.

CONTENTS

Shrink

Give me a shrinker of heads.
Shrink mine. Make it
a pinhole camera
with views of the country.

Make it a padded box
just big enough for a child's head.
Draw dark curtains across its face.
Cut small holes, for views of the stars.

Make it a foot-sized piece of earth
where purple marsh flowers creep.
Make it small and safe enough to sleep in.
Give it views of mountain tracks, green and vertical.

Make it compact. And airtight.
Let nothing out or in.
Make it as unassuming as plastic.
Let it be passed around. Let it be patted.

Give it a kind word.
Let it forget.
Give it the kiss of a black dog.
Give it another cigarette.

Let it be tragic. A song of despair.
But make it short. And to the point.

Sisters and twins

I had the gift of wrongness
thrust upon me. My sister
oldest, tallest, always the bestest,
strides around the garden in her boots.
Magnificent. A born king.
My twin her fragile, chilly queen.

They are the most alike. Fine
faces. Appropriately thin.
I'm standing slightly to one side,
ridiculous. Square. A ballet dancer's
frock that doesn't fit. Bad hair.

The daffodils are finished off
in strangled clumps, with string.

A lesson in twins

It's their doubleness I dislike.
Bad enough the sullen innocence
of one. They smell of eagerness.
Too clever by two halves. Godless.
Matching frocks run up from old
curtains. Shoes with too much sense.

They must learn to separate.
I let the bad one go. The other
sulks, climbs on a chair, clumsy
stands there for hours, hating.
Humiliated. There is hope for her.
She is martyred with a certain flare.

Daddy's smoking on the monstrous arms of a cloud

and there's a man in the bushes going
chip chip chip like a bird sipping dog-coloured water.

Where are you mother? Picking blackberries
and winding up your hair.

It's me taking the wheelbarrow out –
I've filled it with raspberries to look like insides.

I'm wheeling it out with songs for the baby
who's asleep on the concrete and no sisters
anywhere.

Moving

Because the baby was at home
I could make the baby laugh,
I try not to put safety-pins through her skin.

In the new house bare floors,
wasps' nests, hole in my bedroom roof,
telephone upstairs. I keep my animals
in a cubbyhole in the wall.

Because the baby was at home
I could make the baby laugh,
I try not to put safety-pins through her skin.

We went to look at the cold foundations
not expecting a flood. It was when I was
oldest, I saw things swimming
and what if the freezer explodes?

Because the baby was at home
I could make the baby laugh,
I try not to put safety-pins through her skin.

In the new house bare floors,
wasps' nests, hole in my bedroom roof,
telephone upstairs.

Doll

In our snow bunker, doll allows only an eyelid
of sky; she knows I was born facing backwards –
how I long for the truth of the known, red dark.
She says she can change me to her own shrunk shape.
Today we are dressed up for hunting, in our animal boots,
with a rope and a knife. Doll listens to ice, sniffs
the papery air. I walk in the pattern of her passing.

I have left the fibreglass curtains behind
and the vast blue linoleum. This is not sisters,
nor cherry tree, not smashed glass, nor dead fish,
not a scream too loud for a ten-year-old's head.
This is doll who knows I am someone else.
We will charm the gold plastic fish from the tarn.
Our porcelain dogs will look to her.

Dog has risen

Heat has undressed the blank wall
where music comes from.
He can't stop smiling
waltzing through my door like Billy Graham

only made out of paper.
We do the little dance of ghosts
in an accidental twilight.
He still has a nose, a blanket.

He asks for a saucer of water.
When I tell him the lie he says
he heard it spoken in a past life –
the Big Farm in the Big Country

green and green and sky.
We don't talk about killing.
He tells me he works for a living
rounding up the sacrificial sheep

sitting at god's left hand, not biting,
all the wafers he can eat.
We time the creeping darkness together.
When he asks about my life

I can't tell him what warms it.
The child leaping out of him.

Only animals

(for David Hart)

Dog is on the graves
heading for the sea.
He does not mean to be
an instrument of god.

He will not stop
at the red telephone box.
He is fearful of misunderstandings,
also of wooden effigies
of bowls of fruit
of plastic, generally.
He does not care for eagles
nailed to the sky
wings like doors, opening.
He does not care for open doors.
He eats stones to keep his stomach clean.

There is a TV talking
in the hedge, saying
what is it that you want
to a small group of children.
Dog wants to go there.
He is not allowed in.
He doesn't make pictures.
He doesn't neglect his children.
He doesn't rest his head in the fire.

The sea is sucking a sun
into its stomach.
Dog walks on tiptoes
smelling roses.
He knows he is sometimes mistaken
for love, he doesn't mind
the blue boat
the yellow stone moon
the sky's open wound speaks to him.

Last day, Llanbedrog

Dog won't lie down
never mind rescue sailors.
How did those beach huts
get to that car park
in those colours?

He says,
I'm browned off with abroad
I like to go fishing with my friends.
His voice is a fish, lying down.

The mist falls down and up.

I hate to see the mountains as breasts
but sometimes they are.
They are also blue paper cut up.
The violets are here, clean as coal.

The tin man has gone downstairs
leaving his boots full of ashes and freesias.

I will miss you, daddy.
If I go back to the house
will you help me, daddy –
will you?

My mother's house

My mother's house was the sort of house
where dogs sat at table and a whole pig
was roasted for no reason at all.

The servant walked round in old boots
mending our cuts with a blunt needle.
Father always touching his cap saying
lovely job, lovely job.

We had gold in Copenhagen, all tied up
and owed to a man, who was to hang in the park;
I remember watching him smoke a last pipe,
take off his apron and remove his own head
with his genuine, Leatherman knife.

Natasha's house

The men were de-icing the windows of their tanks
but what caught my eye was an oil-drum full of flour.
I thanked the flour for it's nakedness, kept checking my pockets
for money, no money, just Natasha's address.
Lorries going past full of rope.
Smell of the biscuit factory getting louder.

Natasha's house was small and broken,
a motorbike helmet with eyes growing grass.
Where they lived, a fireplace, empty, a poster of a woman
in a dress made of flags. She was holding up her hands
which were red, as if painted. In the burnt-out kitchen
two women were shouting, one was Natasha,
covered in flour. I took her outside.
Silhouettes of planes were passing the moon.

I believed we'd bleed their violence right out of us,
if only Natasha would take me in.
I would have walked all night to watch her hunt –
it was her desperation.

We didn't watch television, preferring maps –
she liked me to curse the places she hadn't been.
When I think of Natasha, I think of the field she lived on,
how it fell from the lip of the valley like glue, how
I wanted to swim in that field with Natasha,
holding Natasha, weak with the fumes.

Natasha's shoes

How glassily you're speaking this morning,
Natasha, putting your black hair behind you,
putting your shoes on.

Don't beat me with your delicate eyes, Natasha,
don't beg me to brush your floury hair.
I'm opening the door to the shining mountain,
striding off in my soldier's heels.

Ice-axe

I watch the men below, marching by the river,
their eggshell heads cold-naked,
blood seeping from their boots and gloves.
Soon the snow will peel back from the steeper slopes
and they will come higher. For now,
the icy fossil fish which decorate the rocks,
the wind which has me on all fours, will keep us safe.
For now, I'll lick your wounds, cook mountain soup
of hawks and ravens, spoon them through your quaking teeth.

Why pull my bare wrists to you, sadly?
They're aching with the silver you'd have bought me.
Remember when you smelled of bicycles and red potatoes,
we crawled to your bed with spikes of saxifrage in our hair.
The sting of our dressed skin made me cry.
I clasped your giant's head as we camped beneath
your table, your nose seemed a whole person,
your mouth a red bucket to capture my desire.

Why speak of shame and fear?
When they come, I'll close your big, brass eyelids
for you, put on your birthday tie.
I'll stop up our cave with a boulder of ice.
My axe is well sharpened, all glad in the sun.
I'm ready for their bombed-out faces,
for their hardcore souls to come.

Apricot

Here can the widow walk, before seven,
on the lawn, soaking her black clothes
under the sprinklers, taking her shoes off.

The widow has painted her toenails black.
She is not allowed to eat.
She wants to take a lover and damage his heart.
She wants to cut the apricot roses and stitch them to her skirt.
She always keeps one hand free, for the chance
that someone might take it.

The widow has left her children behind
in the dark house with the television
with the motorbike and the yapping dog.
She knows they will forget to eat fruit,
to peel snails from the windows,
to boil the water.

But the sprinklers are cooling her skin,
the roses are stitching themselves to her hem,
the house of the famous writer will soon be open.

Federico plays dead
(for Jan and Cathy)

As my gypsy's blood retracts
to the blood of a still moon
and camellias blot my hair,
I breathe caves and cracked earth.
I want the taste of the irrigated earth
of oranges like small suns and bells
and a slow fountain.

I want my human love, who has gone.
The sun's death.

I would lie like this as he lowered
his breath to lie on my skin like a bird.
Each hair raised up by his lips,
his weight pressed down. His kiss.
The place where we meet
is a place where darkness swings
and men walk in, watching
each other's fingers.
Where I long for snow,
for a well to fall into
or a horse, huge and rushing.
My veins are swimming
with desire's lone fish.

There is no courage without him.
I can hardly walk along this street,
where blossom falls on stones and heads
and eyes like tongues are flung against us.
I am cut down, face down,
tasting vomit and spit.
I hear the sprouting of olives
the running of blood

and *Federica, Federica*
a voice like a child,
not like knives or glass,
like the echo of depth.
Like the planting of trees.

I am a man, a girl,
a red camellia, opening.

The birds are holding their breath.
Who will breathe first?
I am flatter than a snake,
blacker than the drumming of ants.

My mother is not a tall building
casting shadows.
My father is not a sprig of asparagus
flowering.

I am a girl, a man,
a red camellia
opening and shutting.

What happened

Cat, of course, was dead by then.
So I chucked her in. I know she
shouldn't have floated, but float she did.
Her fur was like mouldered paper.
The water roused itself and Cat went down
saying nothing.

I never liked her. He brought her home
smiling from his huge, rough hand, unblinking.
She liked to skulk on stairways, made me fear
my own dark corners, the kitchen-table
where I live, mostly. I am my own enemy.
Even the tea leaves snigger.

All summer long she dragged
her barren body from room to room
screaming for it. I'd be in the kitchen
talking to myself, fingernails tap tapping.
Eyes blooming aubergine.

He's never known the difference between talking and fucking.
Likes to use his fists for both.

That night the wind was muscular.
Everything was on its way to somewhere else.
Cat was in the corner, mourning for her
late, charmed life. His hands were in my head
as I held her neck, quite tightly. There was,
as they say, no struggle. Even my gunmetal
heart stopped croaking. Said darkness.
Darkness and deliverance.

Now I put the kitchen-table behind me.
My world is my narrow bed. At night they hit
the window from outside, a mass of feline faces,
eyes like spaceships, weasel fur all flattened on the glass.

And sometimes it's just him.
Wrapped up snugly in an old
potato sack. His big, soft body
bump bumping on the glass.

My lover with her long hair

My lover was what you might call
a nice sword, well intentioned, but
inclined to slice your head off if
dawn arrived too early or too hot
or if you told her a strange dream.

My lover needed a lady, waiting, a lady
for mornings, someone to smooth out her hair,
clear up the night, put her clothes on very gently.

I couldn't do it.
I smelt decay when she woke.
I wanted to plait her long hair
and wrap it round her well intentioned throat.

Thomas in the garden

He wore a long coat, which was black and clean,
his fingernails reached to the ground.
Even in summer, he wore his long coat, his smokeless
white teeth and his genius heat.

Audible night rain. Our park bench leans back
into middleclass bushes, there is no one around.
His long hair is soaked with his pure boyish light,
and black cats are gathering under our clothes.

In fact, he lived with himself as a Christ,
unbearably pure, unbearably wrong.
But I was there, and he wrapped it around me,
his beautiful black coat, which was long.

Amsterdam with Lottie

I have not slept for fourteen nights
lying on the edge of Lottie's reckless life.
Her love is so unspecific, her hands so aristocratic.
Right now, she is writing letters to her
nine most recent affairs.

This room is as sparse as our words.
There's a dressmaker's dummy, unamused,
bare wooden boards. One six-foot mirror.
One double bed. I'm swallowing lust
in gulps of Dutch coffee and chocolate on bread.
At midnight we stumble out into foggy air.
Our insomnia, at least, is shared.

Crack-heads read the papers as we cycle down Haarlemmerweg.
At every corner mist wraps us up like flies.
Amsterdam is England, only strange.
The same dismal rain. The comfort of fog horns
as ships pass us on the watery streets.
In Vondelpark plaster statues are up to their knees.

Lottie, meanwhile, navigates at high speed.
'Pick a bar, any bar!' – walls the colour of oozing blood.
In every corner voodoo dolls glare down
as only voodoo dolls could. A woman sings
until her pimp walks in, drags her out spitting backwards.

And later, much later, not even having kissed
we wade the sober tramlines to the city's edge.
Our bikes whisper beside us in the dawn's freak flood.
Lottie is the scent of canals, of lavender
and grass smoked. I am a small ghost fading,
loving for the last time without hope.

This horse

(for Laura)

This horse is not a rocking horse
with pea-green feet
or nostrils like the flushing lips of shells.
It sings not from the hill of angels

nor talks, nor rocks me to sleep.
Instead, a bed to sit astride
and let my hair down on.
Its coat is ragged gold and ink

it smells of burning gorse, of vanilla
and of heat. It makes a distant noise –
the clatter of bone on air.
This horse is like the muscle of the heart.

This horse comes rushing out of clouds
that speak of storm, is blessed by fields of women.
It sings like hills of kissed skin, the sea is moving in it.

It springs directly from the black work of my heart.
This horse is like the muscle of the heart.

Back there
(after Brendan Cleary)

Well, I woke up that morning in Weston-super-Mare
in bed with a man I met on the pier
(2 A.M. West Country time).
We had fondled several flagons of beer
and I'd followed his blurring words
like a dog needing home.

He held my hand in the maritime museum
and we looked at boats, as if looking at boats
was in our blood. We passed an old man
making maritime notes who looked like
my father, young.

Now we're in this violent afternoon together
and I can't wear my yellow dress and I won't
go out. He says *you haven't found
your sea-legs yet*, but I can't stand the smell
of human mess and he takes a long time to say
my father died at sea.

I thought this could be where I came from.
I thought the bracing air would do me good;
keep me from the mental institutions.

Handkerchief

Foggy, pale blue, late June night,
evening primrose stretching.
Around the land, dim flames from caravans,
Criccieth's inferno of light.

Don't talk to me about immovable feasts –
there aren't any.
I'm running on slivers of marram grass
dark slicing my soles like ham.

Dog jumps in the dunes like a kangaroo.
Dog with his flowery handkerchief.
We've turned into moons, lighting the lace
of on-the-wind-sailors

who die in absent blue waves
and bird sounds flow from the yellow reeds.

Horizontal

Everything underneath – shall I say heaven? –
is low, cloud crawling down mountain.
Only the sounds of Hebog, Rhinog, Moelwyn
and Mawr. Sky and sea such a conflict of grey
the seabird's gold knives may be needed.

Verticals? Only a fine line of heron and dog's
diamond ears, velvet-stroking my hand.
He's been humming since dawn, now
he takes us to silence, wanting no purpose,
the damp heat is dragging my soul.

Shall I lie underneath these thoughts of
who are you? your wrung-out song swallowed,
your silt heart slicing slyly through mine,
when only the blueness returns and the hills,
you, my stone-one, never will.

Coastal park, August

Dog says:
what could be better than anger?

What does he know –
peeing on gravestones,
biting the sea.

What I say is:
thank you god for the aluminium factory,

thank you for the broken shells to dry me,
if only they were a mouth if only on the dark path
you had overwhelmed me.

Small poem

All day I have had your astonishing limbs in mind.
You could so easily be a tree.

Can I walk down from the hill of four pheasants
now I know what it means to be chasing the sun?

I could be forest-dweller, lie at your roots.
I could kiss every soft mile of bark,
let all the fire-leaves fall upon me, until I find

       who made you for me
       but keeps me from you?

Making something of it

October is a birdcage cover over the head.
I crouch in the bath for days, taking in water.
My hair is a beach, shedding empty crab shells
brittle spikes of sea holly. Bones of fish.

The apple tree is sickening.
Honesty rattles its bleached ovaries.

I can't go out. The streets are full of babies
with big faces and girls who carry their bellies
like riot shields. I convalesce in flatness

here where the s-bends of canals repeat themselves.
Tolerance sticks to my feet like peat bog.

I dream of living on cabbages and nettles.
On cold mornings hugging sheep, warming
bloodless feet on the blaze of steaming rowan trees.

The sentimentality of it. This is what we get.
The sea an ice-black wall. Showers of freeze-dried
dog turds whistling through the dunes. Wailing babies.
Women with their eyes and brains scratched clean.

Say

Say you took yourself to the ugly house
and found it locked and darkness falling.
Would you wander in the rockery,
dodging headlights from the road below?

Say you found a garden shed stuffed
with ancient tools and then a woodpile
with a roof of plastic, floor of earth;
comfortable enough. Would you make
a nest to sleep in and patterns of the things you took? –

drugs, prescribed and illicit,
miniature penknife, blunt.
Travel alarm, emergency whistle,
the famous writer in print.

Would you wait in a sort of winter,
forgetting horsetime, forgetting home,
and dream along the violent street
which crawls with burning babies,
muzzled dogs, catch your thoughts –
this time, this time, fate,
please meet me on a windscreen.

Are they looking for you?
          No.
Are they following you?
          No.

You can't go back to cures and solace;
God won't leave you alone.
God, tormentor, never asleep,
would you take your beggars bowl
and his malevolence – and go?

Dog's gift

I've waited by this door for several hours,
my face is changing to grey,
the coldness of the hard surfaces
is seeping into my small, symmetrical paws.
I'm not seeing the dark stairs,
I'm not going back to sit in the fire.
I have made circles of the garden
at high speed, a noose around my neck.
I have done the barking thing.
They think they know my thoughts but there are plans.

The moon is throwing giant in-me shadows
in the blueness of the room.
I am next. I will not be seen.
They'll listen to my heart
and hold my trembling black wool head
to keep me from leaving,
make me lie in the dark with children,
take notes on the direction of my fur.

If I want to bring it to an end,
if I want to go back to the stream
and put my nose under water,
if I want the thigh-high grass
and swarms of gliders overhead.
If I don't want to think about shoes
or the thoughts I had the night before,
I'll become acquainted with this box of matches.
I'll be a user of tools, put my flame to the beds of roses.
I'll give them a burning bush, this dog's gift.

Night in the Dayroom

Let me be inside my soft, brown blanket –
I want to inhabit a creaturely form.
I will be tree-owl, all tented, whilst outside
the night weather falls.
Don't make me fly to my hospital bed,
my father's dead body lives there;
soon, the night nurses will nail pills to my clothes
and here come the scissors to chop off my hair.

Let me see in the dawn on these brooding, black chairs;
outside the ashtrays have filled up with water,
the road is a lake I know I could walk on, but I cannot
describe the damp drill of small wings after rain,
or translate the visions at the back of my head,
my dark head, my hurt head, my head with cracked windows.

Where is dog when I need him?
Out hunting rabbits with his shiny companion,
in a dark field, a bright field, a field wearing two rainbows.

Paper baby

On Tuesday
after a force-fed tea
they gave me a paper baby
all my own.
She burned in my hand –
a love letter.
They took away my treasured knife
and gave me a paper baby
but she doesn't breathe.

The distinguished Dr Chen mutters
patient, how's your sex drive?
I reply, patiently, how's yours
Dr Chen, Dr Chen
father of my baby.
I know you recognise the dreadful
newsprint of her cheek.

Poor paper baby
from dark to dawn she tries to feed
but I can't seem to fold her right.
I keep her in a bedpan by my side.

Even she can't stop me eating glass
or spitting out the ravens
but she helps the barrenness,
she helps the barrenness
my baby, my baby
my paper baby all my own.

Dog and the bad dream

Will I ever awake and will dog ever say –
you know how to climb the sly scree of the mountain,
you know how to walk in the red blade of daybreak.

Dog, in this dream, sucks his cheeks to a skull-face,
a square-headed man is feeding him poison.
Will I ever awake and will dog ever say –

remember the joy of the obstinate peak,
remember the path getting steeper and harder
you know how to walk in the red blade of daybreak.

In this dream our green space is torched to a moonscape,
packs of rottweilers march past like stark soldiers.
Will I ever awake and will dog ever say –

remember the Christ made of glass on the lake
the call of the bellbird, the tree fern's soaked feathers,
you know how to walk in the red blade of daybreak.

I, meanwhile, am sizing up door frames
searching for knives to take to my jugular.
Will I ever awake and will dog ever say –
we'll walk out together in the red blade of daybreak.

Spell for most occasions

Leave your womb task, your shelter task
your strange-in-summer red tree.
Learn from cockroach and magnolia
the careful eating of storms.

Ammonite ammonite
instruct us.
Sacred weeds
inspire us.

Be house with tree
be hill with tree
be gate with tree.

Accept the terror of ending.
Speak the terror of the everyday.

Sea potato sea potato
stay with us.
Godlike worm
sing to us.

Be not invisible
be not invisible
be not invisible.

Feeling better

I'm feeling better so much better now
those thin-eyed geese who have been
flouncing down my vertebrae
have found a different reason
for the flaps of skin between their claws

(now that that there is no water),
they have found a way to let me go,
have settled down to sleep
and I can see that they are gentle,
very kindly yellow to their hearts.

Have no fear.
Sickness is as arbitrary as desire.
I feel well enough to make my bed
and wring their necks and eat and eat and eat.

Allotted

There is nowhere else she can be, except here,
pulling up a chair, in the blue shed made of old doors,
on her ramshackle, rented piece of the earth.
Here is her rhubarb, pink with compassion,
her bird friends, her squash flowers crawling yellow and starred.
Outside, rain makes a cave of her, a perspex sun
is warming her spine. If she sweeps the floor
it will only make her cry.

She must go out to the glorious vegetables,
sink her arms to the elbows in dirt, yes
earth herself up and make her purpose groping for light.
She will push up umbrellas, small and greening,
protected by brambles like coils of barbed wire
and dog, who will lie in the hollow beside her,
barking at hardboard and peacocks and fire.

But when she goes home, will she be safe
from the grins leaning into her wide-awake bedface?
Will she drink water, will she eat food?

Lev. I

We're surrounded by chemists
all flashing their green crosses.
I hate it when the shutters go down
with their shuttering sound
and the circling planes are less like satellites
more like beasts.

You'd think we were surrounded by christ.
I can see the corner of Elbow Street
and the neon blue madonna who
won't jump, no chance,
she wants the black cars to arrive
the godfather to arrive
the rest all smoking, waiting to pick up their suits.

Lev II

In Glen's café the women understand about mothers
and eating brisket with mental nurses.

This afternoon we will all find the divine
in hoover bags and fireplaces.

A secret party of blackthorn trees
will be carrying handbags full of rain.

The man downstairs will be in trouble
with his concrete birdbath strategy.

Lev. III

I'm an attic full of radios
awake until the sky fills in.
Tense cloud again no air
windows open sex rushing in.

Since I touched your electricity
I'm eating elation.
The radios seem to like you.
Magpies cackle their total devotion.

Lev. IV

It's the fear of stumbling out
craving your outline.

I'm already climbing walls
with no rope or hat or hammer

your blankness inside.
Let me meet your bed

I want to lie like
your well-spoken girls,

just leave your soft Italian
slippers on the side.

Lev. V

Long rain, stirring things.
I can't find sex around here
not the sex I want.
Someone walked past before
with a head full of red screwdrivers.

Lev. VI

Community service on Greenbank fields in hard rain,
picking up plastic alien heads.

From here, Levenshulme could be round,
the barbed wire terraces a birthday cake frill.

Dog stay away from the death tree,
don't eat the carnations strapped to its trunk.

Dog greets boy in torn raincoat,
walking small black pig.

Lev. VII

A boy in his *New York Unite* white baseball cap
(no mask) shoulders a brass knapsack full of arsenic.
He is spraying the health centre barricades
his arm pumping up, his back bending over
the folded up maskless white garden boy
weighed down by his brass knapsack widow-maker.

Lev. VIII

New fold-out bench, winking with rainlights,
sky shredded on the ground.
Lamps on in the Blue Bell, early.

Home to a car park and magpies
like algebra. Winter tree floundering,
wrecked wren in the gutter.
The man with rigid teeth, downstairs,
says you must know the water meters.

Shutter speed

She runs into the morning which is melting
to a ragged map of winter, autumn, winter.
A frail sun is rocking on the high tide of the field
but her mind is moored in yesterday
when by fate or chance, she met him in a pine wood.

He was leading lines of children and when he saw her
reeled them in like wayward fish;
she was photographing water.

And no, she never told him of her fool-girl longing
to be taken to a budding wilderness, where animals
are free to speak their minds and safe to wear
their own clothes proudly;
and no one lies alone and withered
on a summer lawn, staring at the buzzard sky,
dizzy with their fevered love affair with death.

And when he speaks, she holds her head above the wave.
And when he holds her to his bear-with-sun-returning warmth

she doesn't cry.
She lets him go

and sets her camera to look long and long
to catch the moments passing in the patterns of the river.

Red house

Pint at the red house, sea like green milk.
The barmaid wants to know how to make shandy,
and crisps? Yes, plain. Bench and table facing the sea.
O the people from the city like a sea-break around me

that's my boat out there, blue and white, see it?

His daughter is describing fish straight from the sea.
She thought it were dead, she stabbed it right through.
You've not tasted fresher

that's the one blue and white out past the dinghy

They're just back from abroad, their hotel was good –
very quiet, very peaceful, you don't mind the muggings

it's just like home, but safer

Change the sheets every day, the towels every other;
make the forecast good and we'll all go out fishing.
It'll be good for fishing on the milk green sea

that's it blue and white, the one with three windows.

Mattress Man

I call myself the ghost of joy
for want of something better.
I do not tend the field, I do not mend the glass
or take the tractor out. Water is difficult.

My friend the mattress man teaches me
the language here but I forget.
Joy. Field. Tractor.
He is fat and also beautiful, arriving on his motorbike,
his fishing-net a flag to greet me.
He thinks of nettles as divine.

Once, in a moment of clarity,
we caught a cloud of butterflies,
invited them in. Were we not blessed
when they settled on our heads
and on the mattress he embezzled for me?
Sometimes he stays, sometimes not.
My body makes the most of him.

The mattress man likes to dance flamenco
with much duende. When he's not making treacle,
he's brewing beer (I like a nice demi-john).
We are so familiar with the moon
and all her phases we merely say, hello moon.
Sometimes I use different sounds.

There are always sounds of work here.
Up at the house they mow the lawn
and cut the trees, repair the roof,
make art sometimes.
Me and the mattress man
are always in our present selves.
We live amongst forget-me-nots
(forget me not my mattress man).

We do not mind decay or growth.
We do not judge the dead or dying.
I am, as women are, a tree, taking the air, enduring.
My man can make a virtue out of thorns.
We live almost in a state of joy.

Esta noche

Esta noche sees us searching the streets
for coffee or tea, no easy task
in this windswept, dustblown town
where water and heat are in short supply.
Looking up from the mud-stained street
the sky opens out, grazing the iron roofs
and already a thumbprint shadows the moon.

Up on the monument, crowds of Bolivians
with telescopes and tripods
forget this town, this desolation.
Death, dig yourself down in this nothing dust,
we're looking to the sky.
We're looking to this shadow
which eats the moon alive.

A girl flashes past, running from railing
to railing, crying 'La luna! La luna!'
I think I'm holding my breath
waiting for the lights to go out
or the end of the world, or something.

Adobe walls, corrugated roofs, spread below us,
a sulphurous sheet that curves away around the earth.
We're staring into space, where fireworks
like fireflies glide, red, gold and green,
blinked out in this ink-black night.
And above us, this pyrotechnic dream.
I've never seen so many stars or known so few –
the Southern Cross, a planet or two
(I haven't seen the Llama yet).
And La Luna Rosa, flowering, other-wordly.

I wonder if you're looking too
from dear old Inglaterra,
or if you're sleeping with your arms
across your eyes, the way you used to.
I'm not surprised you guard them,

I would too, hugging them to you
like a well kept secret.
Your eyes would eclipse the moon every night
if I could look in to them, just once or twice.

The possum-hunter's lover

On Tuesdays now, I wake up to the smell of fur
and in your bed-space, dream the scar around your
neck where you were clawed, not by my lover's rage,
but by those creature's jealous hands.

The bush is quiet at dawn. The trees have swallowed
birds and moon. You'll be home now, putting up
your guns and jars of poison, stacking traps and warning signs.

Every time I drive the dark dirt road by night,
my headlights shining on their little forms,
I think of your hands stroking my neck
as you whisper – *drive straight at them.*

This way
(for J.W.)

I had been walking lonely by the river
the river going forwards, the river doing well,
an extravagance of willows flowing one way,
then the other, my killing shoes glued to a yellow
English meadow, all the wind, machines and bells,
passing far away and high,

when all I wanted from you my friend, was to be woken
by you early, in our studious hotel, swimming up
amongst our dream ropes to the double-edged flowers.
And watch, with you, a human's careful fight
or dance, outside, flowing this way, then the other,
amongst the stationary cars.

So meet me later, by the ornamental vegetables,
let go of that unfathomable scream, that purple sprout
wedged in your throat; I'll join you questioning
the cabbages, beneath their artful hazel cages,
we'll just go this way, then the other,
in the garden, still and growing.

Hilbre Island
(for Geraldine and Geoff)

I don't know why they took me there,
it had something to do with singing,
something to do with death.

They would not let me see
one of them on either side,
I could hear the planes falling,
one after another, and curlews
and hunting dogs weeping.

A feeling of sinking away from land,
sky becoming fierce.
I don't remember Little Eye
but Middle Eye was grassy.
I thought I could hear, across the water,
the gambling sheds out at Talacre.

I knew we were at sea by the crushing
of the wind and when we
reached the rusting lifeboat station
they referred to it as art.
They told me not to climb the ladder
and not to bother with the sea,
mentioned the tides as they kissed me
and left.

I counted the loneliness, waited for it to hurt,
then opened my eyes to new lights, back there,
the land red and moving, seals lying still on
the heaving sea, calling their seal-ghosts   happy.

The little people

at the amusement park shoulder their guns
and head for the garlic beds to disinfect.
A few anxious guardians stand underneath
the hornbeams, sweating.

The little people are talking about what they saw;
about how they positioned the gun
and why her body flinched too late
and the silence when her head blew in.

In their 4x4's the soldiers go,
back to their little town.
In their 4x4's over the hill,
dragging the bodies behind them.

The little people want to get back home,
to pack their satchels with flour.
They want to eat candyfloss and make up songs
before the guardians put them to sleep.

(after P.J. Harvey)

A perfectly ordinary soldier

In a tiny room under a roof of black tin
a rather dark evening was spinning.
She lay on the floor on her skeleton side
walking her fingers towards me.

I couldn't remember when she last ate;
I could see her bones making holes in the concrete.
When I tried pouring buckwheat into her mouth,
she spat it back out.

Her lower lip was so small and shallow
I had to kiss it. She made me feel like
a perfectly ordinary soldier; habitual –
choking on desire.

Trench

I remember there was a tree
grinning through the window,
a green sun lodged in its teeth.
I'd come from filling a trench with children,
I needed to lie down.

I saw the altar, of course, but
how was I to know it was sacred?
Hunger made me forget to kneel,
my body was knives strung together, suddenly.

Who painted the ceiling like that
as if angels exploded on it?
Who said I was singing as I shovelled them in,
singing and radiant?

Of course I didn't sleep.
Next day, out setting traps for water,
I saw a plane passing hugely over.
Something fell. I thought, there is a man falling.
His hands still clutched at something,
his legs were gone.

He was shouting *friend*,
feared one, twin of my twin;
he thought he was saved.
Christ, he called me, *loved one*,
fell gladly at my sacred feet.

I asked if I could close his eyes
thinking he might feel better.
I wanted to lend him my coat
and the keys to my house.
I wanted us to be closer.

Sometime later, the wind began
with its see-through voices.
I know he heard them, too.
He said *they are beating the inside of my head
making pathways*.
I know that we would follow them, loved one
if we knew how to. If we knew how to go on.

Field

1

How much my coffin is like a boat.
Midsummer. I know because of the green
darkness going through me and death smells like
a dug field. The earth sighs as the spade
pushes it back, covers me up, puts me to sleep.
I can hear candle wax splintering, the flame
breathing in. An owl speaks and it sounds
like someone folding their arms with me inside.

The expression on my face has gone.
There is a tattoo in its place, as if someone
had drawn love on me, gently.
The writing in my head says
be in the well and be glad.
I am glad to slide into the water.
I want to be the field. I want to be the dug field.

2

Everything is made of ink,
even this blind light, the colour of
nothing grown and the smell
of all these brown midwinter mornings
reminds me of love.

Straight lines clatter overhead making
a secret of my face. The writing on my hand
says – no one ever arrives.
I pick up a blade from the street.

In the distance there is a green field,
a jagged hole which should not be there.
I wish there was a ragged song in my head,
a wound that bleeds like a lover

whose body stretches and loosens
the moment I arrive.
I wish you could lead me away from the broken houses.
I want to reach the field.
I want to reach the green field.

Borth y Gest

Two deep rowing boats, five ponytails each
one   and one   and one,
rhyming over shallow water.

Holly tree takes out the mountain
which would have been shapely.

There is a girl, red-running from railing
to sea, crying daddy, daddy,

to a man who has mounted the lime kiln,
is leaning back against sun, sharp and blue,
throwing his arms upwards.

Three colours only

She's basking there before me
on a rock they call The Bitch.
She names the rock *beloved*,
thinks she is in love with it –
the way it curves around her
like a seventh wave.

She likes to watch her bitch wreck ships
and later pick the sailors' sheepish bodies
from the surf and lay them out to dry.
She scatters them like jewels along the beach.
They smell like driftwood and when they breathe
like men and lay their stubbled heads upon her,
she cries, as seas of blood and lemons
flow like hymns right through her.

She is, of course, most painterly;
she hangs her sea-goat's horns
with chalices of paint – three colours only;

first: bursts of sky as blue as cruelty
second: sun with no hands
third: wind that thins the skin.

And this is how she begins;
she sings to herself imagined sadness,
her voice is colour bruising canvas,
at sea they hear her minims
on the blue and jealous air.
They hear her longing play
the afternoon like a harp.

She takes her brush to the simmering sea,
she makes it a glass to see through gladly.
She lies to her lovers like a visionary.

Of the backpack and the soul
(after Jen Hadfield)

So I'll climb the red mountain through a nervousness
of cloud and take my white ice-bones up to the sun.
On my back is the blanket, the bread and the fire
and upwards I go to the wind-skirmished tarn.
The bird of my soul is perched on my shoulder,
the warmth of its blue body kissing my cheek.
It is kingfisher or raven and when we make home
I'll change hairshirt for soft flannel, we'll mend
cracked boots, scuffed feathers, sing plainsong
and hill-hymn, welcome the night with its kissed stars,
its jewel moon, its pink halo of light.

Red hen of Skye

I see them lay my body on the verge like a pillow,
sun passing through my evening feathers,
sun low-stroking my broken head.

I am, myself, at the top of our lane,
soft-reclining on a table of light.
I can see the white fortress stores

at Edinbaine, tractors massing on the
o look another rainbow horizon.
No more scratching a living, Red,

you can practise scales.
No more messing about on the hillside
feeling the grass on your beak.

I am on the verge of missing my feathers.
How will they know me without my skin?
I can hear wind mourn but not feel it,
down at Sligachan, under the broken volcanoes.

Dog at Glencoe

I know that the world is a white rock
and dog and myself camped on it.

Dog who is cow-eared, smeared with flies,
who will not put his head in a stocking

who fell asleep in the v of the valley
whilst I smoked,

who swims in the sharp green pools
and fears none of it.

Dog's claws on the stones are
sharpening their moonfaces.

Maybe, later, the hills will lean their long arms over,
let down their red hair.

Maybe the stove will make coffee
and offer it to me.

Maybe dog will be a circle.

Fish soup

Simmer the bones and heads in salt water.
You may need the pan at the edge of the fire.
During this time you may sit on a rock.
Dog may lay down in the sand daisies.
Don't be alarmed by the weight of one wave
or fish dropping back in the water;
the sun will die down, the hum
from the one boat out in the Sound,
this will be a quiet place, and darkening,
the fish giving up their souls to the soup.

2 A.M.

Is it me or is the moon really touching the water?
Soft dark, soft stars breathing out their halos.
The stillness. The absolute absence of roads.

Do I not turn into a mountain, then?

Breathe in, breathe out, an absolute miracle.
The soft stars are moving the absolute darkness,
the terror is easing. Is this it?